A Path to Healing

Lillie Mae Henley

This book is no substitute for any medical or psychological help the reader may need. Please seek professional help if you and your loved ones find the necessity.

The Healing Way: A Path to Healing from Abuse is grounded in the organic environment of pastoral care, chaplaincy, and ministry as a liberal religious minister. It talks about family dynamics, abuse, recovery, self-care, gratitude, spiritual and emotional growth, and contemplation. What I have done, in a most humble way and from my heart, is give survivors a practical, down-to-earth book which offers hope for recovery.

Front cover illustration is titled "Celebrating Life"

Back cover illustration is titled "I Can Do Anything"

Kindle Self-Publishing

Key Words: abuse, sexual abuse, physical abuse, emotional abuse, verbal abuse, meditation, centering prayer, mindfulness, life-lessons, personal growth, spiritual growth, recovery, letting go, forgiveness.

ISBN: Self-Help 9798447925666

Table of Contents

INTRODUCTION

Dear Reader,

In *The Healing Way* I share with you my journey through a life burdened by abuse. My hope is that my journey and all that I learned will be a catalyst for your own growth. If you are reading this, I know you have the desire to live without the pain of abuse. You have the same desire to live a healthy life that everyone has. I also know you have more courage within than you think. And somehow the courage will give you the ability to take the risks necessary to change your life.

By sharing my journey and all the things I learned, I want to bring you hope. Hope that you can recover from abuse and live a healthy, functional life.

These words and ideas lived within me for a long time. I grew up in a home where dysfunctional behavior far outweighed healthy behavior. Although I learned wonderful life lessons from my parents, alcoholism and abusive behavior were dominant. I grew up thinking my family was the only family "screwed up" and every other family was all right. It took me 30 years to see the reality that **all families** are somewhere on a continuum between healthy and unhealthy!

In this book, I write about behaviors and attitudes which will help you become a **better person**. I am not writing about being a good person. Nor am I saying you will become a person who meets others' expectations. Becoming a better person means to me, and I hope it begins to mean to you:

> a person who is willing to learn new behaviors,
>
> become more self-aware, and
>
> see other perspectives of the pain deep within.

The Healing Way talks about the complexities and dynamics of abuse. The behaviors and practices to learn to become a healthier person. Specific steps for healing and simple, human knowledge which we rarely learn from parents, teachers, or peers.

I had to author this book, because I have experienced and seen the pain abuse brings to individuals, our culture, and our world. From my heart, I hope *The Healing Way* will help you live a more fulfilling life.

Rev. Lillie Henley

Section One talks about abuse in families, how it repeats in succeeding generations, what it does to the innocent and what happens to them. It also introduces the first part of the journey of recovery and describes the family dynamics in a dysfunctional family.

The Elephant in the Room

Section One

From Stephen King, Author

There's a phrase, "the elephant in the living room", which purports to describe what it's like to live with a drug addict, an alcoholic, an abuser. People outside such relationships will sometimes ask, "How could you let such a [thing]... go on for so many years? Didn't you see the elephant in the living room?" And it's so hard for anyone living in a more normal situation to understand the answer that comes closest to the truth; "I'm sorry, but it was there when I moved in. I didn't know it was an elephant; I thought it was part of the furniture." There comes an aha-moment for some folks - the lucky ones - when they suddenly recognize the difference.

Family Is Family

Chapter 1

Abuse Runs in Families

Becoming an abuser is a learned behavior. Social scientists draw a model to show the traits and dynamics of family interactions. Therapists call it a genogram. It is like a family tree, except it has more information than a family tree. In this book I call it a family diagram.

At the end of this chapter, you will find four family diagrams. They show the families for three generations. They also show the challenges and dysfunction of the family members. Anyone can see the unhealthy behaviors.

This first story about Luke tells of a family life which must have been horrible.

There was a widowed man named Luke. He had two sons by his first wife who died young. He had one son by his second wife who died in childbirth. Luke was a pedophile, a rage-filled abuser, and an alcoholic.

Luke's oldest son Hubert was a pedophile, an abuser, an adulterer, and an alcoholic. When he did not drink, he was a different person. But anything could make Hubert angry and out came an enraged, abusive person. He would blow up at the nearest family member, and if it were his son Howard, he would beat him. Howard was the only one who suffered beatings, although from time-to-time Hubert would whip his daughters with a belt.

Hubert never physically abused his wife, Rose. He did not beat his daughters like he beat his son. But there are other ways to abuse your wife and daughters. Hubert emotionally abused, denigrated, and subjugated his wife. The daughters suffered from emotional incest when Hubert behaved as if they were his wife and emotional incest when he would demean and denigrate them.

Rose and Hubert had a joke that is quite funny, but the underlying psychological dynamics reflect the horrible dysfunction in the family:

When they retired, both were eager to take a road trip to Las Vegas. Rose wanted to play bingo and Hubert wanted to see the shows. They went to a circus cabaret with topless dances and all kinds of circus animals on the stage. Rose exclaimed after a few minutes, "Look Hubert, they have elephants on the stage!" Hubert replied, "What elephants?"

There is comfort in the familiarity of family dynamics—functional and dysfunctional. Most people are unaware of how deep and strong that dynamic. It is difficult to see the "elephant in the room."

A Family's Story Repeats

Dysfunctional as well as functional behavior repeats in succeeding generations. If it is functional, great, but if it is dysfunctional, it is destructive. Damaging behavior repeats until it is named and healed.

An example of how abuse and dysfunction run in families:

A woman had two daughters one year apart, Angeline, the oldest, and Catherine, the youngest. She was rearing them as a single parent. Catherine was always jealous of Angeline and competed with her for their mother's affection, in school activities, in grades, and for boyfriends. Years after graduation from high school, Angeline married her high school sweetheart Fred. They lived in the same neighborhood as Angeline's family. Within a few years, they had two little girls.

Somehow, Catherine persuaded Fred to fall in love with her, leave Angeline, and move in. The young women's mother allowed Catherine and Fred to live in a small rental home on her property.

Angeline understandably felt betrayed and was devastated. She could not understand how Catherine could steal her husband and worse, how their mother could allow Catherine and Fred to live on family property, expressing her approval of the couple.

Angeline moved far away to another state and never went home, raising her two daughters alone as a single parent. She never talked about the family she left behind.

Angeline's daughters, Robin, the oldest, and Samantha, the youngest, were one year apart. Samantha, like her aunt Catherine, was jealous of her older sibling. Competing for their mother's affection, in school activities, in grades, and for boyfriends. In Robin's last year of high school, she and her boyfriend Jeff became engaged. Somehow, Samantha "stole" Jeff away from Robin and Jeff asked Samantha to marry him.

What do you believe Angeline did about the love triangle? She allowed Jeff to move into their home and live with Samantha!

Like mother, like daughter.

A Family's Story Repeats Itself

Following are four family diagrams which show how abuse repeats in succeeding generations. THESE DIAGRAMS DO NOT REPRESENT ANY FAMILY I HAVE EVER COUNSELED. THEY SHOW HOW FAMILY BEHAVIOR REPEATS ITSELF, WHETHER IT IS HEALTHY OR UNHEALTHY.

Diagram one shows the family of a widower who has several abusive, predatory behaviors which made growing up in his family hell. There is little chance any child or grandchild would be a healthy grownup.

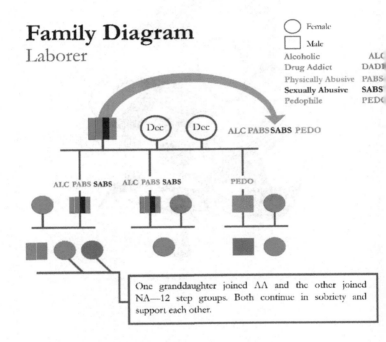

Family Diagram

Laborer

○ Female
□ Male
Alcoholic   ALC
Drug Addict   DADI
Physically Abusive   PABS
Sexually Abusive   **SABS**
Pedophile   PEDC

Dec   Dec   ALC PABS **SABS** PEDO

ALC PABS **SABS**   ALC PABS **SABS**   PEDO

One granddaughter joined AA and the other joined NA—12 step groups. Both continue in sobriety and support each other.

Diagram two shows a mechanic and a teacher who are unhealthy. Physically abusive behavior and alcoholism runs throughout the family.

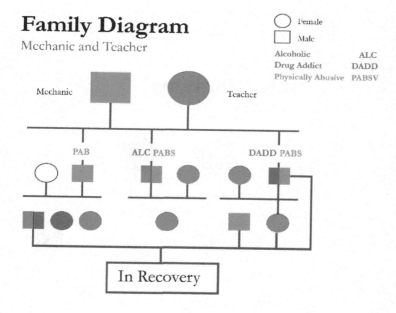

Diagram three shows a family challenged by addictions. Every child and grandchild are addicted to alcohol or drugs. One son is a sex addict. The grandchildren would have to invest in recovery to change the family dynamics of the future.

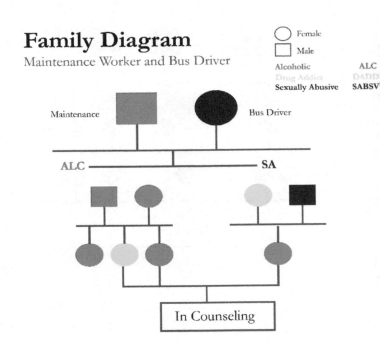

Family Diagram

Maintenance Worker and Bus Driver

Female
Male

Alcoholic   ALC
Drug Addict   DADD
Sexually Abusive   **SABSV**

Maintenance

Bus Driver

ALC ———————— SA

In Counseling

Diagram four shows a functional family with few challenges. There could be many reasons the two grandchildren have challenges. For example, outside-the-family-influences may present challenges to the family, like peer pressure, educational challenges, etc.

Family Diagram
Functional

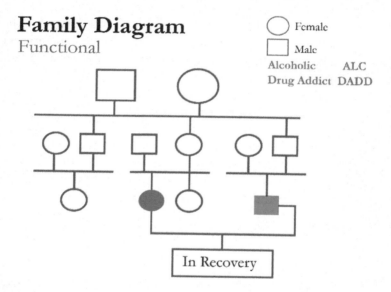

○ Female
☐ Male
Alcoholic   ALC
Drug Addict DADD

In Recovery

Abuse Destroys Self-Esteem, Self-Worth

Most people question their self-worth. It is the rare person indeed who begins life with a strong sense of self-worth and maintains that self-esteem throughout life. In healing from abuse, the first step is to understand that abuse has damaged and destroyed the self-esteem of an innocent human being—no matter what age. Besides sexual abuse and emotional abuse, there are destructive, oppressive, and physically abusive environments that wound and damage more individuals than we can imagine.

> Sitting by my open bedroom window when I was a teenager, I heard the man next door yell at his six-year-old grandchild, "If you don't do that right now, I will stick that broom up your ass." Horrible, I know.

Words are powerful and, in this situation, can destroy a young child. All abuse diminishes self-worth. **Abuse is abuse**. There are no categories which can fully describe the impact of abuse or the depth of pain to the individual.

Abuse Is Abuse

Families — Abusers

Mental health professionals diagnose abusers as people who have all or some of these characteristics:

- think only of themselves
- can love only themselves
- show little ability for empathy or sympathy
- have few morals or understanding of morality
- hold no regard for the laws of society

Sheila was my best friend in the neighborhood. We were quite young, six and seven years old. One day, her family moved. How could I lose a best friend "just like that"? Of course, my mother knew where they were moving. We went to see them occasionally. Sheila and I did not stay in touch, but we never forgot our friendship bond.

As adults, we saw each other a few times, but never met for more than an hour or two. Recently, though, she spent a week with me in my home, and I spent a long weekend at hers. During the visits, we shared some hard truths about our young lives.

She told me the reason they moved to another town was because she confessed to the priest at her Catholic school her stepfather had done some "ugly" things to her. The priest talked to him and within a week they moved from the parish. Her stepfather stopped the sexual abuse but continued to berate and beat all three of his daughters as they grew up.

Another abused woman Deborah told me after she went through puberty, her biological father raped her every morning before he went to work. She grew up, got a job, and rented an apartment. He came over every morning before work and raped her.

How does someone recover from that?

Christina Enevoldsen, author of *The Rescued Soul* wrote:

... someone from an unhealthy family is filled with fear and self-doubt. [They have] ... difficulty with the prospect of life without someone ... The devaluing messages of control and manipulation create dependency so those who most need to leave their family of origin are the least equipped to do so.

Abuse Robs an Innocent of Joy

The Innocent

Every surviving infant, child, teen, and adult are innocent until they are abused. They may at first not understand what is happening. Or in the situation of an adult are surprised, shocked, and terrified. Innocents are helpless and have no power to stop the abuse. Frequently, no one believes the innocent. Girls who develop into young women early suffer abuse simply because of their mature bodies. Abusers and predators sense the vulnerability of innocents. Some children and teens are abused because their abuser give them food and a place to live.

> Years ago, I had a foster son who had a friend from school. His friend lived with a single doctor who supported him. The teens parents had kicked him out because he shared his sexuality with them. It never occurred to me that this doctor might be gay and for payment, the teen had to have sex with him. It hurts me to think I could have done more for this teen, but I had so much pain myself, I did not see the pain in him. Nor did I see it in others. It would take recovery for me to become a compassionate and empathetic person.

Make no mistake about abuse, whether it is the first time or the one hundredth time, the abused are the innocent. No one will ever convince me that an innocent willingly allows themselves to be abused— not even a child or teen who is hungry and homeless.

The Innocent

Chapter 2

How Do I Know I Need to Heal?

- Is there a dark pain within and do I want it to go away?
- Does my spouse treat me with respect?
- Does my spouse emotionally abuse me?
- Do I truly know how to love?
- Do I feel like a "normal" person?
- How does a "normal" person act?
- Do I stay in this relationship because I do not want to be alone?
- Does my anger interfere with relationships and/or work?
- Am I the person I want to be?

These questions and similar ones are familiar to many who grew up in an abusive environment.

Will I Always Be This Way

Look at Hubert and Rose for example:

> Hubert and Rose never socialized with other families, they never had other families over. You know why? Rose could not stand to be around Hubert when he drank, and other people were present. He made a fool of himself, speaking inappropriately around young children and suggestively to any women at the occasion. Hubert's children, as they grew older, were disgusted, and embarrassed at his behavior.

When the family is dysfunctional, they do not socialize with other families, unless of course it is another dysfunctional family. It is difficult for children in dysfunctional families to learn socially acceptable behavior. When the family is as unhealthy as Hubert and Rose's family, so many normal behaviors are missing.

> I was around thirty when I ran into a high school friend at an airport. We had time to sit and chat. Her family, I thought, was one of the "okay" ones.

> Sheila's father was the choir director at a church. As we sat at the airport reminiscing, she told me, "Every Sunday night when we got home from church, my father beat all of us kids. No reason. Whipped us just because."

How could Sheila and her siblings view their experience of weekly beatings as normal family behavior? They sensed *something is wrong* but had no idea how to do anything about it.

Continuum of Healthy and Unhealthy Behaviors

All families are somewhere on the continuum between functional and dysfunctional. We learn to live in our own family's dynamic. Until someone teaches us differently, or we figure it out, we will be comfortable in that environment.

It is a well-known and recognized phenomenon that many mothers and daughters have a conflicted relationship. Perhaps it is more normal than a mother-daughter relationship that is positive and free of conflict.

My relationship with my mother was conflicted. As we both grew older, we could talk without arguing. About three years before my mother Mary Elizabeth died, she told me more of her story. We were sitting around the kitchen table having an unusually deep conversation about girls' and women's lives. At one point she said, "Remember I told you I had a stillborn son when I was fifteen? I delivered at a house way back in the woods. The truth of the story is my Uncle Mel broke his neck as he pulled the baby out."

Mary Elizabeth's story said it all for me. I had no grievances with her after that. Who am I to say to her, "I want you to ask for forgiveness for the way you treated me?" Or, say to her, "I forgive you for treating me unkindly when I was growing up?"

Forgive her for what? Being who she was? A physically and sexually abused girl who grew into a woman who loved a man who emotionally abused her every day of her 40 years of married life.

That one conversation changed my relationship with my mother, and I learned a valuable lesson.

No one is truly all good or truly all bad. We are not born good or bad. We are all born with the capacity to respond to our environment. We behave as we do because we have learned our behavior. Sometimes our outward behavior may be one or the other, for example, mostly good or mostly bad. Never believe that any human being is everything they are on the outside. There is always the Self within who is much more than we can ever know about a person.

What about abusers and predators? They are no exception. However, no matter how much good they may or may not have within, it **does not** relieve them of responsibility for their actions or exempt them from the consequences of those actions.

In Hubert and Rose's family, Hubert was physically and sexually abusive to his entire family. His behavior was deplorable, immoral, and illegal. Unfortunately, he lived in a time and culture where abuse was never discussed nor reported to legal authorities. Hubert never accepted any responsibility for his actions nor faced any consequences of those actions.

Marcia Sirota, psychiatrist, and author wrote:

In troubled families abuse and neglect are permitted; it is the talking about them that is forbidden.

Shush

Chapter 3

Family Dynamics

For me to talk about family dynamics, I must briefly talk about **family systems theory**. I studied the work of two renown social scientists Dr. Murray Bowen and Dr. Froma Walsh. Both are highly regarded in their field.

Dr. Bowen originated family systems theory and Dr. Walsh has authored many books on the subject which include her views of trauma in the family and how it affects the individuals. I will share ideas and behaviors they wrote about which influenced me to believe in my self-worth. These were extremely important for me in recovering from abuse.

Learning about family systems changed my life.

A Family System

No matter our age, everyone needs someone to care about them, hold their hand when they cry, and make sure they are alive and well. And everyone needs a place to eat, sleep, dress, and take care of their private needs. Yet not all families provide such support.

Family systems theory places a high value on the family support individuals receive. One question we can ask ourselves to determine if there is any support from someone in the family who reared us or in our family today:

Q: How do I know ____ loves/loved me?
A: If there is love from the adults who reared us,   we know it in their behavior and actions.

I know Mary Elizabeth loved me because she taught me how to bathe and brush my teeth. When I had a scrape from my bicycle or skates, she doctored me; when I was sick, she nursed me. And she put tuna sandwiches in my school lunch when I asked for them. She hugged me every day.

The only time I thought my father Morgan loved me was when he was sober. As a child he frightened me, and as I grew older, it took everything I had not to hate him. Yet I know in his own dysfunctional way, he cared about his family.

I can now say he did the best he could with the knowledge and experiences he lived through. Like many abusers, he was never held accountable for his behavior. Nevertheless, I do appreciate the good things he taught my siblings and me.

For instance, sometime in our early school days, he taped up a newspaper clipping on our bathroom mirror. It stayed there throughout our growing-up years, and it impacted all three of us.

> To laugh often and much; to win the respect of intelligent people and the affection of children, to leave the world a better place, to know even one life has breathed easier because you have lived, this is to have succeeded.

It is ironic, isn't it? Morgan was an abuser who had enough "goodness" in him to guide our lives toward **some** positive outcomes. The quote attributed to Ralph Waldo Emerson may have been what Morgan wanted from his parents. I do not know. I do not care. All I can say, for Mary Elizabeth and my siblings and me, the goodness never outweighed the harm.

Family of Origin

Our family-of-origin is supposed to take care of us and care about us. Unfortunately, this does not happen for everyone.

Facing the Future Alone

Ronnie Musgrove, inspirational speaker, and writer

> After my father died when I was seven and my mother entered into an abusive relationship, I shuffled between houses – staying with friends, families from church, and relying on the kindness of teachers and people throughout my commu-

nity to help me grow up essentially
without parents.

There are all kinds of families in all kinds of living situations, ranging from palatial penthouses to small mobile homes to homelessness. Abuse permeates at every socio-economic level in our culture.

The crucial belief we must have if we are to heal: We are not the place where we live and we are not the people we live with. We are someone with the potential to create a life we want to live.

It is helpful to find a person who will support us on this journey. It can be a single family member, or it might be a teacher, a caring neighbor, a mentor at work, or your therapist. It is hard to do this work alone.

Support Can Save the Innocent

Section Two shows how to begin the journey of recovery intentionally and purposefully. Creating a vision, becoming a grateful person, and learning to be contemplative are at the very beginning of the recovering journey.

Section Two

Laurell K. Hamilton wrote in Mistral's Kiss

There are wounds that never show on the body that are deeper and more hurtful than anything that bleeds.

Eleanor Roosevelt, activist, politician, egalitarian

In the long run, we shape our lives, and we shape ourselves. The process never ends until we die. And the choices we make are ultimately our own responsibility.

Chapter 4

Abuse completely, irrevocably, changes you from who you were and could have been to a person struggling with a dark pain inside and no insight of how you can be. No matter how or when it occurs. From infancy to adulthood the darkness of abuse remains, even when it is blocked or pushed deep within, until the light of recovery begins to shine.

Create a Vision

The first step to healing is to see yourself transformed. In psychology and other fields which study human behavior, researchers have agreed, when a person can see the successful completion of a task, they are more successful at achieving their goal. To heal from abuse, be open to your imagination, your spirit, your desires, and your need to feel whole and pain free.

Most importantly, be open to the change recovery brings. Ask yourself these questions:

- Do I want the pain within to go away?
- Do I know how to love myself?
- Do I want to feel and act like a "normal person?"
- Do I have anger that comes out of me over which I feel no control?
- Do I have other issues that affect my life in negative ways which I need to resolve?

These and other questions are all normal questions innocents have. A technique which helped me see myself as a better person is guided imagery. Guided imagery is a story written, not to entertain, but written to help the listener see herself as a healthier, better person. I wrote this guided imagery especially for a journey of recovery.

It works this way: you read the story into a recording app on your phone. Read it slowly and thoughtfully. Then find a quiet place where no one will bother you, find a comfortable place to sit, relax, and open yourself up to the words you have recorded. There is also a recording at www.lilliehenley.com

Guided Imagery for Visioning a Healthier Person

This guided imagery is written for a female perspective. Men and non-binary should change the words to fit your nouns and pronouns.

RECORD THIS GUIDED IMAGERY

Relax. Breathe deeply, open your imagination to this journey. See with your mind's eye. Breathe deeply, slowly. Imagine yourself in a room. Walk around. There are windows on all sides. The windows are open, and you feel the breeze of the wind flow into the room. You can see a beautiful world out there. Water where you could get your feet wet or swim. Do you smell the fresh water?

There are diverse kinds of trees and many shades of green. Oak, pine, cedar, and fir. Can you smell the fragrances coming from the woods?

Look at the water. Can you feel the energy of this beautiful body of water? What about the energy from the earth? There is energy all around you, from the water, from the earth, from the life-giving bright sun.

Turn around and look at the room. When you look at the furniture it says, this is my room. I am safe here, every molecule of my being, every aspect of my Self is safe.

Breathe deeply, slowly. Find a place to sit. It is comfortable and exactly right for your body. Feel your body sitting. Feel your arms at your side. Your hands are in your lap. Feel your legs going down to your feet. Feel your feet on the floor. Feel your whole body sitting quietly in this beautiful room.

Breathe deeply, slowly. Imagine you see a woman near the window. She looks like you, but she is a healthier, happier you. It is you that has gone through all that you have gone through **and** will go through. It is the beautiful, serene, compassionate Self you are to be.

Look closely. She loves herself. She has serenity, compassion, peace, love. She has confidence and courage. She finds herself being at peace throughout her day.

When challenged, she becomes still and discerning. She does not react. She embraces what is happening and responds with kindness and compassion.

She is the recovering you. She is the evolving you, the becoming—better you.

Breathe deeply. Reach out your hand and take the sunlight streaming in through the window and wrap it around your hand and send that powerful energy to your becoming self. It is the *energy of the universe. It is the light of the universe. It is the love of the universe.*

Now, you want to send her serenity, love, confidence, and courage.

You say, I do not have these to send her. Yes, you do. All these ways of being are deep within. You were born with them. Dark pain hides the best of you.

Reach out again with your hand and take the sunlight streaming in through the window and wrap it around your hand. Sweep the dark pain inside with that light and see how it transforms dark pain into light energy. This light energy gives you the strength you need to become the person you want to be—whole, at peace, and filled with a quiet joy!

As the dark pain transforms into light energy, you see more of your beautiful self. You see the aspects of serenity, *love, confidence, and courage.* They are all there.

Send them to your becoming self. Serenity, love, confidence, courage.

Breathe deeply, slowly. Take as much time as you need to embrace all these ways of being within you.

Breathe deeply, slowly. 20 SECOND PAUSE

Sit here for a while. Allow the sunlight to flow over you, allow the light to flow into your Self transforming the energy of the pain into the energy of joy. You are creating a beautiful, healthy Self, one step at a time. Sit still, very still, and continue to look at the woman you are becoming.

Breathe deeply, slowly. 20 SECOND PAUSE

You can come back to this room anytime you wish. You can see your transforming self every time you take a step of recovery. Practice this guided imagery as often as you like.

Now, come back to the present. Slowly allow yourself to embrace this moment. You are back where you need to be.

Chapter 5

Be a Grateful Person

What does it mean to be a grateful person? A grateful person is one who is thankful for the amazing and ordinary things that make up our lives every day.

Doctors diagnosed a man I knew with cancer. As he was battling the disease he said at one point, "I am grateful that I have cancer." He is not the first person to say this to me. What those cancer patients mean is with a diagnosis of cancer, they have an opportunity to re-think their life. They fight the cancer, but they also have a chance to explore what is important in their lives. They focus on their relationships and their purpose. These are the some of the most grateful people I have ever known.

Years ago, I had a friend who kept a gratitude journal. I asked her if she discovered anything about gratitude. She said, "I've found out that there are more things than I realized that happen to me every day for which I am grateful. Things that I never recognized as something for which to be thankful."

Many friends and acquaintances who have gone through troubled times, depression, and loss of loved ones have told me, "Gratitude saved me."

Here are gratitude exercises to practice every day. They can be silent or spoken. As with all the advice in this book, make everything work for you.

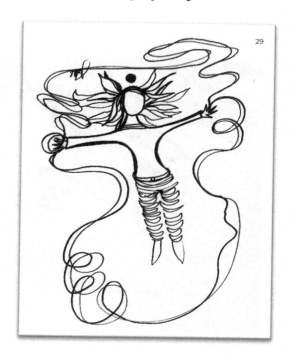

Every time you open your eyes from sleep, say to yourself or aloud:

I am grateful to be alive.
It is another day where I can choose
to improve my life.
I am grateful.
I am grateful I can get out of bed and walk.
I am grateful to breathe.
I am grateful for those who love me.
Add any other gratitude …

From Farm to Table to Soul

When you sit down to eat, say to yourself or aloud:

I am grateful for the hands who grew this food.
I am grateful for those who prepared this meal.
I am grateful.
I am grateful for the ability to feed myself.
I am grateful for this glass of water.
I am grateful for this time to eat.
I am grateful for this time to be mindful.
Add any other gratitude ...

When you are around people who support you say to yourself or aloud:

> I am grateful _____ is in my life.
> I am grateful _____ supports me.
> I am grateful _____ loves me.
> I am grateful for co-workers who support me.
> Add any other gratitude …

Every time you close your eyes to sleep, say to yourself or aloud:

> I am grateful for my life.
> I am grateful for ____ which happened today.
> I am grateful for the those who love me.
> I am grateful for the *grace* in my life.
> Add any other gratitude …

Often during the day, I find myself grateful for my work, when others are kind to me, when someone hugs me! I find myself grateful for each breath, for the ability to walk, for clean water. There are hundreds of things each day for which we can be grateful.

Being intentionally grateful in everyday life will change your life.

Chapter 6

Be a Contemplative Person

A contemplative person is one who is peaceful and composed. Someone who quietly goes about life with open eyes seeing not only the surface matters of their environment but perceiving or sensing what lies behind interactions and behaviors. A contemplative person is serene.

Two of the most unhealthy and dysfunctional behaviors visible in my life were anger and drama. More than anything, I wanted serenity and tranquility but had no clue how to achieve it.

Being contemplative means healthy behavior and no drama. No arguing, fighting, screaming, hateful emails—no toxic behaviors. If there is a disagreement, a contemplative person tries to respond with healthy behavior. They will try not to take part in unhealthy relationships.

Survivors must learn a healthy response to drama and highly charged negative behaviors.

How Do I Respond?

Try this:

Take a moment when faced with destructive, dramatic behavior and be still. Yes, simply be still. It works wonders — stillness. It conveys the message: "I am here, yet I will not participate in an argument with you, and if you continue your raging, your yelling, your denigrating, I will walk away." Wait a moment, then walk away.

Of course, the person showing these behaviors is unhealthy. They may not allow you to walk away, holding you by physical force. If they threaten harm, you must run away.

However, I am not talking about a life-threatening situation. I am talking about a person in the family, at work, or in any other aspect of life, who responds to events with drama and aggressive remarks. At that moment, it does not matter what is going on in your mind, we will discuss this later in Section 4. It is imperative **to appear** serene, collected, peaceful when drama rears its ugly head.

Learning the external behavior of a contemplative person is a crucial part of your journey. Have you ever heard the saying, "Fake it 'til you make it?" The urban dictionary defines it as:

> To act like you are something so you
> can, in fact, become that [some]thing.

When Life takes you to places far from where you began, you must find a way *to be* in that environment. Jill, a survivor and a friend of mine, grew up in Louisiana on a farm. Few people in her life had a high school education. She, however, accepted a scholarship from a very prestigious east coast university. She had to learn how *to be* among highly educated people. There was nothing in her background that could have prepared her for this environment. Well, I say nothing, but being well-mannered and amiable she discovered was a good foundation for a new way of being. After her undergraduate degree she was offered an opportunity to study at another well-known university for a doctorate. She had to learn how *to be* in the higher echelons of academia.

This lesson is critical, and I will repeat myself. When Life takes you to places far from where you began, and especially if you are a survivor, you must find a way *to be* in that environment.

I tried to explain this to my brother when we were in our thirties. He had no clue *how to be* because he was an innocent. He did not know how to present himself outwardly as a confident, caring person. He had to learn. He had to "... act like ... the someone he wanted to be so..." he could become that someone.

Ways to Learn Serenity

How does a person become contemplative? I struggled with anger. I knew I had to find a way to be serene. Finally, I tried meditation.

Pushing Busy Mind Away

There is so much more to meditation than just sitting, breathing, and trying to clear your mind. Millions around the world practice because the benefits are priceless. You can find the benefits of meditation on thousands of websites. The Mayo Clinic website shares the science behind it. The list below is from the Mayo Clinic website. https://www.mayoclinic.org

The emotional benefits of meditation:

- Gaining a new perspective on stressful situations
- Building skills to manage your stress
- Increasing self-awareness
- Focusing on the present
- Reducing negative emotions
- Increasing imagination and creativity
- Increasing patience and tolerance

Most importantly, meditation teaches stillness and serenity. If you have doubts about meditation, set them aside for now and open your heart to contemplation and serenity.

Meditation, Centering Prayer, and Mindfulness

There are three prominent schools of contemplation. I use the word *contemplation* to emphasize all three are paths to serenity. However, people use the word *meditation* when referring to any of these three schools.

Contemplation helps a person realize there is something *other than* or *greater than* every day, ordinary life. The *other* and *greater* could be many things. It could simply be a peaceful state of mind when your everyday life is chaotic and stressful. Or meditation can lead you to an attitude of compassion for others. The *greater* could be a faith in something greater than humanity. Contemplation can lead to a belief in the values of Buddhism or the principles of the Baha'i faith. Simply put, it can lead to an awareness which cannot be experienced in daily living.

Meditation has roots in Hinduism and Buddhism.
Centering prayer has roots in the Catholic Christian tradition.
Mindfulness is the most recent tradition, having roots in the twentieth century. In each tradition the intent is to let go of the ego and the busy mind.

Meditation is the practice of being still and breathing purposefully, watching the breath enter and watching the breath leave the body. *Watching the breath,* feeling the body move with the breath, is one of the most important aspects of practice in all the schools of Hinduism and Buddhism. The purpose is to empty the busy mind and experience the bliss of solitude.

Centering prayer is different from meditation in that the purpose is to empty the busy mind, let go of the ego, and open oneself to the experience of a divine presence. The practice brings one to a place of stillness. Centering prayer uses a word that is *sacred* so when the mind wanders, saying the word brings one back to stillness.

Mindfulness is the practice of becoming aware of the *present moment*. It helps develop self-awareness. The practice itself is rooted in the ancient Eastern philosophies. Today's mindfulness movement developed over the last five decades from research by teachers and scholars of University of Massachusetts and Johns Hopkins. The practice leads one to a place of serenity and peace.

Learning and Living a Contemplative Life

There are those who have a healthy surplus of energy, a lot of things on their mind, and believe they are temperamentally ill-suited for meditation. There are busy, distracted people, and even people with attention deficit hyperactivity disorder (ADHD) who think meditation is impossible. They make these and similar remarks: "I'll never be able to let go of my busy mind," "Meditation isn't for me," "I just cannot get my mind to cooperate!" Because I am borderline ADHD and thought I would never be able to meditate, I had to find a way to learn meditation that worked for me.

I began meditation practice for one minute at a time. Yes, one minute at a time! There are people who practice and teach meditation, but I have never heard them teach, "Learn one minute at a time." How do I know it works? Because it worked for me. In the beginning, knowing I wanted to be a composed and serene person, I began with the attitude, "I'm going to do this no matter what it takes."

I began by stopping what I was doing at any time during the day. I took a deep breath and said to myself, "Relax." I did. And then I went on about my business. I did this a few, then several, then many times a day. After a few weeks of this I thought that all those moments of "Relax" must add up to something.

So, I began to stop myself, take a deep breath, and relax for a few more minutes—about three. During those three minutes I told myself to forget what I am doing and focus on something. I focused on gratitude. If any thought entered my mind besides gratitude, I would shush it away! I was learning how to stop and relax, but not yet meditate.

After a couple of months, still at about three minutes of relaxing and focusing on gratitude, I added the most important aspect of meditation: watching the breath. At this point I let go of my focus on gratitude and began to focus on my breathing. Teachers say, "Watch your breath flow in, watch your breath flow out."

For this a person visualizes the breath coming in and the breath going out with the movement of their lungs. Some easily learn how to watch their breath, but for others it is difficult. It is visualizing the in and out of the breath through the mind's eye. Watching the breath takes practice. And we finally get to the word practice. For everyone, whether a guru, a yogic, or a person who watches her breath for only three minutes, watching the breath is a practice.

For months I practiced watching my breath for three minutes at a time. To be candid, this three-minute practice may be enough for some. Practicing this several times a day may accomplish what a survivor needs to be—peaceful, serene, calm. For me, I needed more.

Beginning a Path of Practice

Today there are thousands of audio books, e-books, books, and podcasts available which teach meditation, centering prayer, and mindfulness. I read books on Buddhism, Hindu yoga, centering prayer, and mindfulness. Below are my favorite sources of reading and listening. Some give explicit instructions on practice, some invite you to contemplative reading, some talk about the rich traditions of meditation.

Authors I have read and recommend:

> Cynthia Bourgeault
> Eckhart Toll
> Henri J. M. Nouwen
> Jon Kabat-Zin
> Pema Chodron
> Thich Nhat Hanh
> Thomas Keating
> Wayne Dyer

Following are excerpts from three popular authors on meditation, centering prayer, and mindfulness.

Meditation

Dominique Atkinson in *Meditation: The Beginners Guide*, "Basic Breathing Spiritual Meditation"

To master … meditation, it is important to understand that there is no past or future. Time is an illusion of the ego that keeps our attention away from the present moment. Why would our ego do that? Simply because when the attention is focused on… the present moment the ego does not exist.

When we let go of the illusion of time and focus only on the stillness that is in the present moment, we find who we really are, beings of pure spirit who know love, strength, clarity, light, peace, and joy beyond anything that we could create in life.

Centering Prayer

Cynthia Bourgeault in *Centering Prayer and Inner Awakening*

It's ... [quite] simple. You sit, either in a chair or on a prayer stool or mat and allow your heart to open toward that invisible but always present Origin of all that exists. Whenever a thought comes into your mind, you simply let the thought go and return to the open [silence]... You use a short word or phrase, known as a "sacred word," such as ... "abba" (Jesus' own word for God) or "peace" or "be still" to help you let go of the thought... You do this practice for twenty minutes, a bit longer if you'd like, then you simply get up and move on with your life.

Mindfulness

Jon Kabat-Zinn in *Wherever You Go There You Are*

It is all too easy to remain on something of a fog-enshrouded, slippery slope right into our graves ...to wake up and realize that what we had thought all those years about how life was to be lived and what was important were at best unexamined half-truths based on fear or ignorance, ... and not the truth or the way our life had to be at all.

No one else can do this job of waking up for us, although our family and friends do sometimes try desperately to get through to us, to help us see more clearly or break out of our own blindness... But waking up is ultimately something that each one of us can only do for ourselves. When it comes down to it, wherever you go, there you are. It's your life that is unfolding.

Places to Learn

There are temples, spiritual centers, yoga studios, meditation centers, monasteries, convents, and ashrams where you can learn and practice. There are also groups who gather in homes and social centers for practice. In the beginning, it is easier for most people to learn from others.

I learned at ashrams and temples around the Chicago and Washington, D.C. areas. Everywhere I traveled, I looked for a meditation center or group, and there was always a place to learn. Now I am a solitary contemplative, finding my peace and serenity in practicing alone.

You may find new things happen to you when you seek ways to learn:

- Another way of life and new friends. People who are healthy and functional, easy to meditate with who enrich your life.
- Ways to meditate that are unique to you and easily adapt them to your way of life.
- Your own path to being a contemplative.

Remember, the goal is to become a contemplative and serene person.

Going Within to Come Out Transformed

Where Section Two helps develop stronger character traits and greater emotional and spiritual depth, **Section Three** suggests ways to heal through education, counseling, and support groups.

Section Three

Oprah Winfrey

Think like a queen. A queen is not afraid to fail. Failure is another steppingstone to greatness.

Chapter 7

Healing Through Education

Where Do I Begin?

When determining the health or strength of a family system, social scientists look at how much education each member has. You might ask what education has to do with family health. The more education a person has, the greater the chances they can achieve a better life for themselves. Of course, there are no guarantees

in life. For human beings there are always challenges. Education, though, makes the individual stronger and more able to confront whatever life presents.
Having a better education also means our world becomes larger and our dreams more achievable.

What else does a better education mean? A person without a high school diploma could earn a GED (the equivalent of a high school diploma) and apply for better-paying jobs or to college. Someone with an associate degree could go to college and find opportunities in a world she only dreamed of.

There are thousands of educational opportunities on the internet. Schools offer online courses, and not just colleges or universities. There are cooking schools, gardening and landscaping schools, and retail management, for example. There are unions and associations that teach people how to work. State employment agencies and sometimes county governments will help. There is federal money for women who have been homemakers. There are federal and state resources for former military. In addition, there are podcasts that offer advice and websites that offer training.

Near my home in Mexico, there is a smokehouse run by a young man. His ribs are as good as any I have ever eaten, and I have had ribs all over the South! One day I asked him how he learned to smoke and grill such good meat. He said, "I learned how to barbeque on YouTube!

Nelson Mandela

Education is the most powerful weapon...
you can use to change the world.

Education transforms us. We may not recognize right
away how we change, but we do. One thing is certain:
no one can ever take away our education.

Chapter 8

Healing Through Counseling

Counseling was my first step. I know that counseling is not for everyone. Some of those reasons may be:

- Insurance does not cover counseling.
- No insurance.
- Fear of sharing deeply with someone.
- Fear of uncovering "the truth."
- Fear of what others may think.

If financial resources keep you from seeking a therapist or counselor, there are many U.S. communities which offer therapy at no or reduced charges. Search on your county or city websites. There are also counseling practices that give reduced charges to individuals. Do not give up because of money.

If fear holds you back, it is a strong challenge to becoming the person you want to be. I will talk about fear in Section 4. Fear is primal. It is in us to protect us from harm. The value of talking aloud to a trusted counselor far exceeds the value of whatever fears you have.

Audre Lorde, Black poet, activist, second-wave feminist

When I dare to be powerful, to use my strength in the service of my vision, then it becomes less and less important whether I am afraid.

Forfeit Fear to Find Me!

If Counseling Is an Option

Find a counselor who understands your pain and challenges. They must be able to relate to your determination to become a healthy, functional being. Ask friends about counselors and therapists they may know. Try to find one who specializes in families and/or abuse. Do not feel committed if they do not inspire confidence. Look for someone else.

Developing trust with the counselor is primary. Once established, it is imperative to share your innermost fears and highest hopes. Trust me on this. For a long time, I did not share some things that were happening in my life because I did not think they were that important. I was very wrong!

When I went back to university in my thirties, I had a friend working on her undergraduate degree who was around my age.

Summer, grew up in an abusive family environment, went back to college in her early forties to get her undergraduate degree. Like so many of us, she had doubts about her intellect and self-esteem.

What was great about going back to college was the counseling service her school offered its students. She found a school counselor she trusted and went to her for the two years it took her to finish her courses and graduate.

She performed well in college, making the dean's list every semester. In her senior year, the Senior Women's Honor Society invited her to become a member. And Kappa Delta Pi, one of the largest and most prestigious educational honor societies, invited her to membership. Still, she continued to wonder if she was smart. However, I can say, her self-esteem had grown in those two years.

Something happened right before she graduated. Her advisor asked, "What are you going to do after graduation? Move to Vegas and be a dancer?" Why would a professor ask such a question? Did he think it was funny? Was he a predator or just a nasty old man? Summer looked at him as if he were crazy, gathered her papers and left.

What she came to understand is even though she had grown emotionally, she had a more work ahead. Was there something in her behavior to prompt a professor to ask that question? Maybe. She did not stay in his office to ask him why he said that, and the answer would not have been helpful to her.

Summer continued counseling after she graduated and got a job. She found a therapist who specialized in Adult Children of Alcoholics and family abuse.

Her story is our story, and our story is her story.

Chapter 9

Healing Through Support Groups

How do you find a group?

If you see a counselor or therapist, they should be able to tell you about different groups they know of, or even ones they facilitate themselves. Your counselor may be in a practice with other professionals who facilitate groups for recovery from abuse.

Be on the lookout for notices pinned on bulletin boards at bookstores, coffee shops, recreational venues, churches—any kind of meeting places where people meet. The kitchen where a group of us gathered each week to cook a meal for the homeless had a bulletin board. There was often a notice of a new group forming for healing and sharing stories.

There are more places than you might think for individuals to meet and share stories. Sharing stories helps individuals in the group heal. Keep your eyes open, and you may see a flyer pinned to a bulletin board at the back of the grocery store!

Or you can start a group of your own with the help of a professional counselor or therapist. The wounded can help the wounded; however, there must be a mental health professional in your group who understands the participants and their issues. You want nothing harmful to happen to anyone in the group, and a counselor can intervene if someone in the group shows unhealthy behavior.

"Unlocking the Past"

Chrystal shares her story:

"Sitting in a group meeting facilitated by my therapist I heard a woman talking about her abusive brother and suddenly I hyperventilated. My therapist asked, 'What is happening, Chrystal?' I saw herself as an infant, pre-toddler age, and saw my step-grandfather above my stroller. He pushed his finger inside me, and I cried. It was *the moment* in my adult life I realized the abuse began when I was months old.

"One day, when I was fifteen, my brother started to rape me, as he had done since I was eleven, and I grabbed a knife from the kitchen and told him, 'Stop, or I will cut you.' He knew I meant it. Later he had me bring home girls from school who liked him, and he would rape them.

"All along, I kept everything my uncles and my brother were doing to me secret. By the time I was in my early twenties, I had blocked it all. Deep down, it was still there. I would let no man touch me.

"I never said a word to my mother about my brother and my uncles. I thought I was the bad one."

After a meeting, I was standing around in the parking lot talking with the other women, and someone said something—a word or a sentence about her feelings—and suddenly, whatever was changing inside me, started moving. Anger split my chest open, and pain spewed out of me like a cloud of red matter. I was the only one to see this spiritual manifestation of what was coming from deep within. I knew at that moment that I was healing. The pain and anger left, and I was at peace for the first time in my life. This happened because I trusted the members of the support group and I allowed myself to share the worst with them.

Anger Split My Chest Open

Chapter 10

Healing through Journaling

Writing Moves You Forward

Writing in a journal is extremely challenging work for some of us, but for others it comes as easily as breathing. These people, once they begin, sometimes write for many years. Some of us can write every day in a journal for a week, or a month, or for six months, and then put it down and not write again for months or years. I have learned helpful and healing things by journaling on and off for years. Who knows if I would have healed sooner if I had been more faithful to journaling. All I can say is, "Everyone in their own time."

If you decide to try journaling, look at your everyday life and ask yourself, "When would be a good time to write in my journal every day?" If it does not look like journaling could be an everyday affair, then pick 2 or 3 times a week to journal. Try to make your journaling a sacred part of your day or week.

You can buy a journal, or you can use a spiral notebook. Put the date at the top of the page and begin writing. Write anything that comes to your mind. You can set a timer for as long as you want to write, or you can write until you want to stop. When I say you can literally write what comes to your mind, that is what I mean.

Remember, journaling is a very private, intimate act of self-expression and healing. You are the only one who needs to read your journal. Although if you want to share something from your journal with your therapist, it might help.

The best therapist I ever worked with said, "Journaling is the best therapy you can do, better for you than all the therapists in the world!"

Section Four

Below are quotes by famous two women who knew more hardship than most of us can imagine. Both encountered deep suffering on their journey through life.

Lucille Ball, greatest comedic actor in television

... nothing can be changed until it is faced.

Frida Kahlo, word renown twentieth century Mexican painter

At the end of the day, we can endure much more than we think we can.

Section Four is my favorite, "Simple Human Knowledge" filled with information we rarely learn. Few people think to teach the thought processes behind their behavior. We see it but rarely ask about what thoughts preceded their behavior. Unless we take psychology in college, we rarely hear of this learning which we need to be mature, healthy, better people.

Chapter 11

Visions of Hope and Change

What's Missing? Simple Human Knowledge

What many counselors and therapists do not share very often are simple human truths that we all need to learn. If we are from one of those families that were not very healthy, we learned little social conventions, or cultural norms or social ability. They do not teach the information you find in this section in school unless you take psychology class in college.

We will explore some fundamental truths about human beings. This information is necessary to become a mature, healthy, functioning person. For many, these simple human truths are new information.

How Does the Brain Manage New Information?

As we grow and learn, our brains associate new knowledge with information we already have stored. A good example is math:

It is easy for children to learn to add and subtract. Teachers introduce and relate it to experiences of the young ones. Next is multiplication and division. The brain connects it to the arithmetic already stored. Math is progressive. After the basics, its multiple functions, then algebra, geometry, advanced algebra, trigonometry, and calculus. All building on the earlier courses.

What happens when exposed to entirely new ideas? It is difficult to learn that information because the brain has no previous knowledge to connect it to. For example, in a basic seminar on computers for the administrative staff of an information systems company, the programmers introduce how the computer works. It uses two numbers, 0 and 1, called a binary code.

For the administrative staff who deal with words, documents, and files, it is difficult to understand, unless they have already had a computer class. Or if they had advanced math in school. Administrators' education focuses on accounting and administration. There may be no prior knowledge for the new information to attach to! How To Learn New Information?

Information, like the ideas explored in Section Four, may be entirely new. There may be nothing to relate it to. If so, be intentional and use your imagination. Read carefully. Imagine pictures in your mind's eye which can reinforce the reading. Look for familiar words. And read key sentences aloud.

Create a place in the mind's eye that can store the unfamiliar information. It may look like a file folder, or even a file cabinet or a book where you add the pages. Imagine any object that will help keep this information.

Psychologists call retaining or keeping information **internalizing**.

However, unless the information changes behavior, that is all it is—information. When the information alters behavior, it becomes part of the individual's value system and guides their actions.

Psychologists name this process **integrating**.

A simple example of internalizing and integrating information:

If your mother takes you on her motorcycle for a pleasant drive in the country on Sunday afternoons, you will see her check the tires, the gas tank, the oil, and the brakes. When you are younger, she does not explain too much of what she is doing. As you grow up riding behind her, you will learn many things about the motorcycle simply by listening to and watching your mom. If, by chance, you like the idea of having your own motorcycle when you are old enough, all the knowledge you have from listening to and watching your mother becomes internalized, it is the foundation for the new knowledge you will gain as a motorcycle owner. By the time you are old enough to get your license, you will have internalized everything you have learned over your growing-up years. It has become part of your value system.

There is a movie I have watched more than once, *The Ramen Girl*. It tells the story of a young woman who must create a new way to see herself, to live, to work, and **to be**.

Abby (played by Brittany Murphy) flies to Tokyo to be with her boyfriend. She arrives; they spend one night together, and he leaves her for a job in another part of Japan. He does not plan to return, does not ask her to go with him, leaves with a remark like, "I didn't think you'd really come to Tokyo."

Devastated and alone she goes to a neighborhood ramen shop. Not only does the bowl of ramen ease her emotional distress, but it brings her back to the shop for more ramen. Eventually, she quits her job and begs the ramen chef to "Teach me ramen!"

Chapter 12

Differentiation

Despite years of therapy, I had never heard of **differentiation** until a few years ago. A friend who had been a counselor for over thirty-five years told me about differentiation and said, "It is the hardest human behavior to learn."

Learning to Differentiate Is NOT Easy

How are we supposed to learn differentiation? What is it?

If we see two people, Jan and Nancy, having a disagreement. Nancy brings drama into the conversation and Jan stays calm and peaceful. We do not know for sure what is going on inside Jan's head, but we see the results. Nancy stops the drama because Jan refuses to take part in the drama.

What Is in Our Minds—Anger—Calm

Differentiation Happens in Our Minds

Before any further exploration of differentiation, I must explore the busy mind with you. I cannot count the times someone tried to explain to me the busy mind. Here is an explanation that will hopefully add meaning to what you already know.

The mind likes to be the primary thinker. It likes to tell us what to do, all the time. To control our thinking, it continually looks back and brings up memories. Often the hurtful ones. It gets more attention with those. Sometimes it brings up the good times. The busy mind shows us all the things we need to do, images of things we want to do, even fantastic ideas that are not relevant. "Surely, the future is more exciting than what is going on now."

Try this exercise. It is an intentional way to find out what the busy mind is up to. Do this several times a day until you realize just how the busy mind works. It is always working!

Several times a day, **stop** what you are doing and pay attention to what the busy mind is thinking. Surprise! It may remember an event that happened five years ago, or it might think of something to do next week. It never stops, **unless** there is a way to make it stop. If you pay attention, you will notice how your busy mind tries to be the dominant character in your thoughts.

A neuroscientist said something like this: "Truly our mind is not our friend."

Our busy mind controls us. If it were up to our busy mind, it would rob us of the most beautiful times of our lives—**the present moment**.

The American Psychology Association's definition of differentiation theory in terms I can understand. Human beings can filter out environmental noises, unimportant information, and even harmful information while allowing essential information to enter the brain. For example, if someone is in front of you shouting and screaming because they are mad at you, it is possible for you to ignore the drama and allow yourself to think clearly in the face of that drama.

Integrating—Internalizing—Enriching

There is more to differentiation than filtering out the negative and threatening. There is the element of being nonjudgmental. In our culture, judging people is a habit. We even judge by standards created by others: advertisers, public personalities, neighbors, even friends. Seldom do we think how negative this is to our lives and to other people's lives. Healthy people try to avoid negative thinking and try not to judge.

Stephanie Carroll, My *Conversations with God Book 4*

> Every time you hear yourself being judgmental, make yourself think something positive, even if it is simply a silent 'bless you.'

To successfully differentiate in any situation:
- Let go of your own anger
- Let go of how the other person' anger affects you
- Let go of judgment
- Let go of insults
- Let go of hurtful wrongs
- Let go of any negative feelings
- Let go of everything that is not important in your life

Letting go is just that, **letting go!** It means exactly what it says. To be healthy, mature, better—learn to *let go.*

When you learn to differentiate, you realize that most situations with drama are not that important in the healthy living of your life. Consider yourself a serene, healthy person and do not respond to drama. Sit quietly and wait for the drama to end. Or leave the room.

Imagine this scenario and how differentiation works:
You are walking into a parking garage. There is a person at the parking ticket machine. And they are screaming, banging on the machine, kicking the machine, etc. To differentiate you "filter out" all the negative energy and noise coming from that person. You walk on, unaffected by their behavior.

How to Learn Differentiation

I learned differentiation by creating mantras. Mantras are a concise list of words that help you focus on filtering out the negative or damaging drama.

I meet a new employee one level below me who tells me when we meet, "I'm going for your job, you know." My mantra:

> Do my job, be myself, focus on the moment
> Do my job, be myself, focus on the moment
> Do my job, be myself, focus on the moment

Another situation where differentiation is helpful:

Say there is a person who spends more than her scheduled time in the break room. This person not only talks incessantly, but sometimes shares confidential information. Somehow, she always gets an excellent review. I say to myself, "I work harder than her, yet she gets a raise this quarter and I don't." All this is upsetting.

Then I think, I do not sign her time sheets or sign the checks deposited into her account. Why waste time and energy on any situation that has nothing to do with me?

It is not my concern. If I am unhappy, and I am going nowhere in this company, I should look at changing my job. Meanwhile, I say this mantra until I can do something about my work environment:

> Focus on my work, focus on my work, focus on me
> Focus on my work, focus on my work, focus on me
> Focus on my work, focus on my work, focus on me

Creating mantras is a life skill developed to filter out the negative actions and behaviors of others. It becomes part of a healthy, mature person.

Differentiation is achievable!

Chapter 13

Fear

Neuroscientists tell us that our brain stem, the oldest part of our brain, is hard-wired to fight or flee when confronted with anything that overwhelms or threatens us. Our brain is ever vigilant, even after thousands of years of development. It instinctively reacts with the warning fight-or-flight response when confronted with a challenge. It can be a conflict with a colleague, an argument with a loved one, or any other situation where we feel threatened.

Note: Some readers may be familiar with recent behavioral studies which add two more human responses: *freeze* or *fawn*. A person will freeze, be unable to leave or respond. Others will fawn, respond positively to the threat. For the sake of simplicity and clarity, we will not address this new research in *The Healing Way*.

Brain research confirms that this hard-wired survival instinct underlies all our actions and behaviors. In our modern culture, we do not need this fight-or-flight instinct as much as in humanity's earlier times, at least in terms of physical survival. But in terms of our survival in our daily lives, our brain continues to be wary of any situations that threaten us psychologically, socially, mentally, or emotionally.

For instance, take a long-standing disagreement between a husband and a wife or between two people who used to be good friends, but no longer speak to each other. Behind their disagreements is fear:

Fear of change
Fear of not changing
Fear of loss
Fear of trust
Fear that the other will see us differently

There can be many reasons for fear. They may be rational or irrational. When we are challenged in any way, our primal brain triggers fear. Instead of a wooly mammoth that wants to trample us, we may now face a person at work who threatens us. Although our brain still signals fear, the healthy way to resolve the situation may not be to fight or flee, but to understand what is going on and try to reach a peaceful solution.

If fear overwhelms and makes it difficult to live a healthy, mature life, it is time to see a counselor or therapist or someone who can help. Fear can keep a person from achieving a better life.

I found a poem years ago which describes the courage needed for emotional and spiritual growth. It is a constant guide for me. Patrick Overton wrote in the Leaning Tree (1975).

> When you come to the edge of all the light, you have, and must take a step into the darkness of the unknown, believe that one of two things will happen. Either there will be something solid for you to stand on—or you will be taught how to fly.

Chapter 14

Resilience

In an American Psychology Association journal, I found an article that defines resilience:

... resilience is adapting well in the face of adversity, trauma, tragedy, threats, or significant sources of stress—such as family and relationship problems, serious health problems, or workplace and financial stressors. As much as resilience involves "bouncing back" from these hard experiences, it can also involve p**rofound personal growth**.
[My emphasis.]

Every human being on this planet faces problems, trauma, and life-changing challenges. It is what we have inside us that helps us respond to life events. It is our inner self. We cannot see these intangible characteristics which make up our Self, but they are there: feelings, beliefs, emotions, personality, spirituality, values, and many others, including **resilience**.

Resilience is one of the intangible characteristics of our inner being. It is the part of our human spirit which helps us overcome traumatic and tragic events.

A woman I knew told me that years before, her fifteen-year-old son disappeared one day. That morning, she said, they made plans to meet at the mall. He never showed up to meet her. She never saw him again. The FBI told her a boy about the same age as her son from a neighboring town also disappeared the same day. She said, "It was more than I could manage. I spent the next two years in a psychiatric care facility." Her counselors helped her reach the resiliency within. Eventually, she came to terms with her loss and sadness and embraced life again.

I did not know anything about resilience until my fifteen-month-older brother died at 42 from an ultralight plan crash. I thought we were twins when I was a little girl. That tells you how close we were. I did not fare well. My manager said I could take off work, but when I returned, he said, "I did not mean a month! I meant two weeks!" I quit my job and found a minimum wage job in a furniture store. Two years! It took me two years to come to terms with my loss.

Finally, I went back to my brother's therapist, and that is when I found out about resilience. He told me, "We may be naturally resilient about some things because it is part of our inner self. But when bad things happen, we can consciously access our ability to be resilient." I learned I could be resilient not only about my brother's death, but also about the abuse, the pain, the anger. I could choose resilience over sadness.

If you look at the definition of resilience above, you will see the last sentence says, "As much as resilience involves bouncing back" from tragic experiences, it can also involve "profound personal growth." And that happened to me. All the therapy, groups, self-help books, audio books—all of them clicked into place in my brain and in my heart.

No, I was not suddenly perfect. No human is perfect. And I still had to learn that I could not **cut out the mess within**. I had to use it for my own "profound personal growth."

There are as many ways to face tragedy as there are people. We all have some degree of innate resilience, but sometimes we must go one step further and purposely, consciously call on our resilience to face the future and engage with life.

After your loss is past and life is settling in again, you will need to decide—this could be days, months, or years—but one day you will have to face your world, changed forever, and decide to reengage with life or continue to draw away from life. Your resilience influences that decision. If your resiliency is strong, it will move you forward to another life. One that you build each day by day by day. Your resilience will challenge you to be better than you were before.

Mary Elizabeth, a country woman through and through, taught me something about resiliency. One day, I asked her, "Mother, how do I go on?" and she replied, "one foot in front of the other, Lillie Mae, one foot in front of the other." I decided right then, I could face each day not knowing what it would be like, because I was tired of feeling overwhelmed. My mantra from Mary Elizabeth:

> One foot in front of the other
> One foot in front of the other
> One foot in front of the other

Chapter 15

Adaptability and Rigidity

Adaptability is the part of our inner being that can adjust to new situations and changes. Another word for adaptable is flexible. The more adaptable a person is, the healthier and more mature an individual.

Rigidity is the part of our inner being that refuses to change! Another word for rigid is inflexible. A rigid person has plans for the day and will not change them, even if a friend comes by on the spur-of-the-moment and wants to spring for lunch. The more rigid a person, the greater the challenge of becoming a healthy, mature individual.

For example:

Suppose you planned a family vacation with two other families. You are the person who took care of reservations for camping sites, hotels, and theme parks. Months ahead of time, one family needed to change the dates because of illness in their family.

> If you are an adaptable person, you will say, "I will try to rearrange everything. Just give me a few days. I'll see if we can do it without losing deposits." You would do your best to make it happen for all three families.

> A rigid person answers, "No, it is all arranged. It just cannot be done."

Adaptable people do not fear change; they accept it, even embrace it, because they know change will happen, no matter what. Rigid people fear change.

This is one of those simple human truths of life that few people talk about and fewer still refuse to admit that they are rigid people. Life gives us the opportunity every day to change. City changes the roads we take to work, our favorite grocery store closes, and our best friend moves across the country are a few examples of changes in life.

Often, I had to introduce change to a church which I served. In the beginning, I would say to everyone, "I'm all for change if it's my idea!" Everyone would laugh. Later, sitting around a table, trying to agree on the change process, everyone who was against the change would give their reasons:

One woman said, "We can't do this, my husband would roll over in his grave!" Oh, really?

A man said, "I'm all for the change, if it doesn't look any different than it does now." Sure!

Once a woman whispered in my ear, "I'll vote for the change, but I'll call you next week and tell you how to do it, okay?" What?

Chapter 16

A Comfortable Environment

A simple human truth. We are comfortable in our family environment, whether it is functional or dysfunctional. If we grow up around abuse, it happens to us. We are in a messed-up family, but we are **subconsciously comfortable** in that familiar dynamic. That is why sometimes innocents never seek healing or a different life.

> Cheryl, the oldest of three sisters, lived in a dysfunctional family where her father was a sex addict. Not only did he insist on sex with his wife two or three times each day, but he read pornography whenever he had the chance. He did not hide his reading habit and left his magazines in the one bathroom they all shared. As Cheryl grew up, she came to hate the sexually evocative atmosphere of her home. She could not wait to grow up and get away. Marrying in her late teens to a young man from her neighborhood who was home on leave from military service. Knowing him most of her life, she hoped he would take her away from "All this."
>
> She joined him on his tour of duty in Europe, excited and away from her home—far away. As she settled in, she discovered Richard was something

like her father. Coming home from work at lunch and looking for sex. As a young bride, she complied, thinking it was her duty. Later, he brought home pornography magazines and DVDs or XXX-rated movies and insisting she watch them with him. It never occurred to her to leave Richard.

They were in Europe for several years, then moved around the world for three years until they returned to Europe. They had three sons. After she had three boys, she wondered about her family environment and how it would affect them growing up.

Why did she choose Richard from all the young men she knew in her life? **Subconsciously, he was familiar.** Like father, like husband.

Fortunately, some innocents figure this out and intentionally find mates and create homes free of abuse. The key word here is **intentional**. The cycle will not break until someone consciously breaks it with determination and maturity.

A simple human truth—all of us are comfortable in the environment we grew up in. When I say all of us, I mean humankind.

Chapter 17

Boundaries

We need boundaries. Not just some of us, all of us need boundaries. It is simple, but also complicated. Children need boundaries so they can learn how to treat each other, their parents, others in their world. Children need to know what their world is, what makes them safe, and what to do if someone violates their boundaries. It is the responsibility of parents to ensure their children are safe within those boundaries.

There are boundaries for parents, too. Parents need to meet each other's needs and must not expect any offspring to substitute for their spouse or intimate partner. Healthy, mature people do not complain about their spouse to their children, nor should they try to gain leverage against their spouse with the children. When there is a blurring of boundaries between parents and children, abuse occurs.

There are emotional and sexual predators who use their children as substitutes for adult companionship and relationship. Were you abused this way and do not even realize that your experience was abuse, destructive, and damaging? Remember, there is no scale which can measure the effects of abuse on an individual.

Boundaries are supposed to keep us safe. They make clear the roles between adults and adults, adults and children, children and children. A mature, healthy adult knows how important boundaries are for our families, society, and culture.

Chapter 18

Forgiveness and Letting Go

The catalyst for this book is the popular cultural phenomenon of forgiveness. Everyone thinks it will all be okay if we just forgive each other. Forgive other countries for genocide, forgive white people for hundreds of years of systemic racism, forgive murderers for killing our daughters, sons, husbands. Forgive predators who prey on innocents. We even forgive young men and women for preying on our children on university grounds, in fraternity houses, and in locker rooms.

I will begin with a novel idea: It is unnecessary to forgive everyone for everything.

When an innocent becomes a healthier person, recognizes the difference between healthy and unhealthy behavior, has integrated these simple human truths into their life and moved on, **do they even have time to forgive?**

They will not care about the abuser(s) who changed their life with a single act or more. The survivor will be too busy becoming a healthier person to live in the past. They may, through mature and healthy decisions, want legal consequences for the abuser(s). **It is the survivor's decision to make**.

Please know I am NOT talking about a rape of an adult or a child that is current, the perpetrator caught, and law enforcement involved. This book may help those innocents on their journey, but the destruction is recent and there needs to be supportive individuals with the adult or child.

Is there ever a reason to forgive the perpetrator? Only if the survivor feels the need. Remember, I said abusers are a diagnosable person who has no conscience, no ability for sympathy or empathy. It is rare for an abuser to have remorse. Generally, someone saying to an abuser, "I forgive you," does not mean anything to them.

Most proponents in the forgiveness culture say forgiveness is for the forgiver and heals the forgiver. I say, learning how to be a better person and living a healthy life, creating healthy relationships heals the survivor.

It takes every bit of one's tenacity, vitality, and resiliency to recover and transform. It takes one's intentional effort to heal the hatred within. It takes courage to heal the damaged parts of the personality, as well as clean out all the plain old dark muck within.

Once again, I quote the best therapist I ever had: "Use all the dark muck within as fertilizer for your growth." She is the one who taught me there is no way to cut it out and become perfect! Since there is plenty of muck, I had plenty of fertilizer!

Who has time to forgive? My mother Mary Elizabeth and I both moved on when Morgan died. We were too busy improving our lives and neither of us ever thought about forgiving him. In truth, we rarely talked about him. Mary Elizabeth was happier the last ten years of her life than she had ever been. I was too busy on my journey to even think about forgiveness.

Forgiveness in Another Light

For the sake of those who hold forgiveness in another light and wanted something else out of this book, I will tell you:

> **Forgiveness** takes all the intentional work I have discussed in this book. When you say, "I forgive you, Mother, for treating me that way for thirty years," you are really **letting go**. Letting go of the negative and hateful. It takes courage letting go of such pain, and I am sure those who let go of the past have done significant work to be able to let go. Letting go shows mental, emotional, and spiritual growth.

The Pain of Letting Go of a Loved One

NOTE: In this segment, I am talking about being in relationship with a significant other. I am not talking about rape and or abuse from a stranger. This is particularly meant for familial and intimate relationships.

What if you live with someone who is a user, a manipulator, or simply too selfish to be in a healthy relationship? What do you do when the pain they cause creates unhappiness? If you love them, how long do you continue to love them despite their inability to have a healthy relationship? Do you *forgive* them every time they abuse you?

You love them until you cannot love them any longer without professional support. Therapist, counselor, social worker—someone you both trust to help you put things in perspective. But since you have already done a lot of work learning and changing to become a healthy, mature, better person, you already know what it will take for them to be a mature companion. Will they do the work? You do not have to *forgive* them any longer.

You love them, but it is not in your best interest to continue living with them. You may love them until you die, but it may not be possible to live with them that long.

What is natural at this point is to wonder, "Why did I stay so long?" Or a million other questions that could lead to a negative assessment of yourself. It is even natural to go through the useless mantra,

> If I would've, or if I could've or I
> should've.
> If I would've, or if I could've or I
> should've.
> If I would've, or if I could've or I
> should've.

You do not have to apologize when you say, "No more. My life, our life together, cannot support, encourage, or sustain me any longer. I must go." When you get there, you will know it.

What is un-natural for us and an extremely hard lesson to learn—we need to forgive ourselves for *allowing another to abuse us*! **I am not talking about someone who is physically stronger than we are. That is another situation all together.** Who thinks of forgiving themselves? I learned this after leaving such a relationship. The **only** person I needed to forgive was me. And when I say, forgive myself, I mean it. Do not just say the words, believe them. Believe them.

Letting Go Is Never Easy for Humans

Chapter 19

What to Forgive?

There are ways people hurt each other in the normal course of relationships. They forget to pick up someone we have promised to take to a party or forget a lunch date. Forgetting to pick up a spouse's formal wear at the dry cleaners and they are already closed. What do they wear to the wedding tonight?

Mistakes and missteps are just what they are, hiccups in our lives. Most are unintentional. A simple, "Will you forgive me?" can overcome hurt feelings and normal anger.

Forgive each other these small, painful hurts.

On my journey, I realized that very few things must be perfect. The engineering of a bridge, the architecture of a high rise, the construction of a ride at a theme park, and surgery. Anything involving risks to life needs to be perfect.

A grocery list, our order at a fast-food diner, our over-burdened waiter at a busy restaurant—these do not have to be perfect. A wedding does not have to be perfect. The most memorable weddings are those where something goes wrong, and the wedding couple laugh so much the guests cannot help but laugh! We spend time and energy on making our homes, cars, and our appearances perfect so other people can see how perfect we are.

Our culture needs to change. But first we must change ourselves! We need to forgive ourselves for thinking we must be perfect. Simply, lovingly, we need to forgive ourselves for all the things we are not responsible for, but which we blame ourselves anyway. Forgiveness must start with us.

Remember, we need to be willing to accept our imperfections, learn to laugh at ourselves, and cultivate a life of joy!

I Create My Own Life, My Own Story

Afterword

You were at one time *innocent*—no matter your age. An abuser destroyed your sense of self-worth. You and only you can heal yourself and become that someone you want to be. You do not have to forgive anyone. Hopefully, you are too busy becoming a healthier, better, more mature person!

As you become emotionally strong, you will find out a simple human truth: abusers are **nothing**. If they need forgiveness, let God forgive them. She is in the forgiving business!

The *innocents* are all around, supporting each other, caring for each other, giving each other hope. **Never be afraid to ask for help**.

I cannot end this book without poetry from an influential Black poet and author of our time—Ntosake Shange. From *for colored girls who have considered suicide/when the rainbow is enuf*:

> ... [the] cruelty that we usually think we face alone, ... we don't. We discover that by sharing with each other we find strength to go on.

Remember this book is for you.

The *innocents* who let go
The **survivors** who are changing
All who are healing and getting stronger each moment of each day of each year becoming a better person.

Gratitude

Like many of you, I began a new path in 2020. What began as a Zoom class on writing poetry and memoirs became this book. The first person to thank would be Judith Campbell, well known author and teacher, who influenced my decision to write what was in my heart. Thanks also to the participants in those Zoom gatherings who encouraged each other and me to write.

Then there are the loved ones who encouraged me, Jean, Cassi, Kelly, Darin. Also, thanks to my beloved friends who provided spiritual and emotional support: Camala, Coco, Eiko, Isabella, Jill, Jo, Leanne, Linda, Lorraine, Melody, Paula, Russ. Last but not least Sandini who gave me the title, as well as her time.

And an incredibly special loving gratitude for Jude Dubé. Her spiritual guide advised her thirty years ago that she would be creating art which, "You must keep for future endeavors." Then, twenty years ago, Jude began her own journey of personal growth and began to draw each day as a spiritual practice. Her art became a source of healing.

Jude lives in the same La Quinta neighborhood in Ajijic, Mexico, as I do, and we have been friends for the last three years. Several months ago, while sharing the latest news of this book, she asked me, "Would you like to see the artwork I drew on my journey of healing?" The rest of the story is evident in her wonderful illustrations. I know her art will inspire you as much as it did me.

Something about the Author and Illustrator

Lillie Mae Henley

Lives in Ajijic, JAL, Mexico, in a charming casita in the LaQuinta community. She volunteers as an egg lady. The egg ladies pack eggs for families in San Juan Cosala. She also helps at the ESL program for all ages of Mexicans who want to learn English. She says, "The best part of life is sharing my joy with others."

Jude Dubé

Jude's casita at LaQuinta is right on Lake Chapala so she sees the fabulous sunrises and sunsets. She believes mistakes are for learning and discovering one's potential. Intriguing conversations, wine, good food, and flowers are her inspiration. She expresses her passions on her canvasses of life and art. She says, "The best part of my life is sharing the candy-of-life, laughter."

Made in the USA
Columbia, SC
11 June 2022